I Feel Purple

A Crabtree Seedlings Book

Written and illustrated by
Margaret Salter

Crabtree Publishing
crabtreebooks.com

Author: Margaret Salter

Editorial director: Kathy Middleton

Editor: Janine Deschenes

Illustrator: Margaret Salter

Proofreader: Ellen Rodger

Production coordinator & Prepress technician: Margaret Salter

Crabtree Publishing

crabtreebooks.com 800-387-7650

Hardcover 978-1-0398-0666-5
Paperback 978-1-0398-0692-4
Ebook (pdf) 978-1-0398-0715-0
Epub 978-1-0398-0742-6

Published in Canada
Crabtree Publishing
616 Welland Avenue
St. Catharines, Ontario
L2M 5V6

Published in the United States
Crabtree Publishing
347 Fifth Avenue
Suite 1402-145
New York, NY 10016

Library and Archives Canada
Cataloguing in Publication
Available at the Library and Archives Canada

Library of Congress
Cataloging-in-Publication Data
Available at the Library of Congress

Printed in the U.S.A./012023/CG20220815

How does the color **purple** make you feel?

You can find the color purple in a lot of places.

makeup
hair

There is a lot of purple in my garden.
Purple makes me feel

HAPPY.

I have seen pictures of kings and queens wearing purple. Purple makes me feel

IMPORTANT.

Sometimes purple can **HURT...**
like when I get a bruise.

I think my favorite purple shirt gives me good luck. Purple makes me feel

LUCKY.

Purple makes me feel **ICKY.**

Mom tried to feed me purple carrots once.

Nope!

Purple makes me feel **INSPIRED.**

What happens if I mix **purple** and **red?**

Wow!
Magenta!

Purple

and white make lilac.

Purple and yellow

make...

brown.

The color of gingerbread!

My bedsheets at home are purple. Purple helps me feel

CALM.

BOO

Purple feels **SPOOKY** to me.
Not scary spooky, but in a fun way.
Like how Halloween is fun and spooky.

Purple doesn't make me feel anything. That's okay.

My best friend
likes purple
A LOT
though!

Sometimes the sunset has purple in it. It's **PRETTY** and **SCARY** at the same time.

How does

purple

make you feel?

Notes to Caregivers and Educators

Colors can link to emotions in many ways. They have different meanings to different people, who have unique points of view. What Color Are My Feelings? encourages readers to be in touch with their feelings and how they connect to colors. Use the question and activity prompts below to guide children in exploring how colors make them feel.

Help children create a color wheel using primary and secondary colors. Then, ask children to assign a feeling to each color. Have them label each wedge of the color wheel with a feeling. Invite children to share their color wheels with their peers.

Review pages 16 to 21. Have children identify the colors made by mixing purple with red, white, and yellow. Then ask them to predict what colors could be made by mixing purple with other colors. Review primary and secondary colors and allow children to experiment by mixing paint.

Review pages 22 and 23. Ask children what other feelings they have at bedtime. What colors remind them of this time of day? Why? Invite them to draw a picture that shows the colors and emotions they feel at bedtime.

About the Author and Illustrator

Margaret Salter grew up in the very colorful country of the Bahamas where she saw pink flamingos, green palm trees, and vibrant blue oceans. Now she is still searching for more colors in Canada.